STUDIES IN MODERN EUROPEAN LITERATURE AND THOUGHT

*General Editor:*
ERICH HELLER
*Professor of German*
*in the University College of Swansea*

# MARTIN BUBER

*Also published in this Series:*

Ian W. Alexander: BERGSON
Arturo Barea: UNAMUNO
E. K. Bennett: STEFAN GEORGE
W. H. Bruford: CHEKHOV
Roy Campbell: LORCA
J. M. Cocking: PROUST
Wallace Fowlie: PAUL CLAUDEL
Hugh Garten: GERHART HAUPTMANN
Marjorie Grene: MARTIN HEIDEGGER
C. A. Hackett: RIMBAUD
Hanns Hammelmann: HOFMANNSTHAL
Rayner Heppenstall: LÉON BLOY
H. E. Holthusen: RILKE
M. Jarrett-Kerr, C.R.: MAURIAC
P. Mansell Jones: BAUDELAIRE
P. Mansell Jones: EMILE VERHAEREN
Janko Lavrin: GONCHAROV
Rob Lyle: MISTRAL
Richard March: KLEIST
José Ferrater Mora: ORTEGA Y GASSET
Iris Murdoch: SARTRE
L. S. Salzberger: HÖLDERLIN
Elizabeth Sewell: PAUL VALÉRY
Cecil Sprigge: BENEDETTO CROCE
Enid Starkie: ANDRÉ GIDE
J. P. Stern: ERNST JÜNGER
Anthony Thorlby: FLAUBERT
E. W. F. Tomlin: SIMONE WEIL
Martin Turnell: JACQUES RIVIÈRE
Bernard Wall: MANZONI

*Other titles are in preparation*

# MARTIN BUBER

BY

ARTHUR A. COHEN

BOWES & BOWES
LONDON

First published in 1957 in the Series
*Studies in Modern European Literature and Thought*
Bowes & Bowes Publishers Limited, London

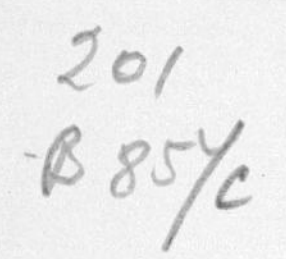



*Printed in Great Britain*
*by Richard Clay and Company Ltd,*
*Bungay, Suffolk*

CONTENTS

Introduction . . . page 7

I. The Bare Bones . . . . 20

II. First Principles: I and Thou . . 37

III. The Bible and Hasidism . . . 59

IV. Man's Way in the World . . . 85

Biographical Notes . . . . 106

Bibliography . . . . . 108

# *Introduction*

In the year of the death of King Uzziah, Isaiah the prophet beheld the throne of God, and the host of seraphim ranged about it. Each called to the other the thrice-spoken Holy. It is then, amid the experience of having seen God with his own eyes, that Isaiah observes his own corruption and unworthiness.

In *The Idea of the Holy*, Rudolf Otto argues convincingly that the development of man's response to God is made in terms of the holy. The constellation of terror, awe, infinite distance, dangerous proximity, and power constitutes the primary phase of awareness. Moses casts the foreskin into the face of the angel of heaven; Moses and Joshua remove their shoes on sacred ground; Uriah dies when he touches the ark. These attest to the activity of the holy—direct, pre-rational, terrifying. God is manifest in the terror of his presence. He is commanding power: he asks of man and he takes from man. It is only at that moment in religious history when it becomes apparent that God not only *requires* but *needs* as well, that his holiness is complemented by his glory. The display of God in his glory is, by contrast to the terror of sheer power, a mitigation of that power, a complementing of that power by an asking of worship and a statement of glory. Isaiah says,

> Holy, Holy, Holy, is the Lord of hosts;
> The whole earth is full of his glory.

Notwithstanding his distance and inaccessibility, the holiness of God breaks through to human perception. The affirmation of glory is a judgment upon the holy, an assertion of man's encounter with holiness. In the fact of the simple worshipper beholding this holiness the earth is filled with glory. It is at this moment in the development of the religious sense that man becomes aware that God may be approached and praised. Not distance and circumspection, but the awe of recognition and participation become manifest. The power of the Holy and the glory of the Holy are joined, for the distance and nearness of God are disclosed at the same meeting, focused through the heart of man, spoken forth as the supernal subject of man's subject. Isaiah speaks these words at such a moment, for God is, as the Hebrew word for sacrifice signifies, being approached.

He is distant and remote, yet accessible and near. The reality of his holiness lies in the fact that it is visibly testified, that the heavens open and a man beholds. At this moment one speaks holiness in awe, wonder, and amazement.

The history of the holy is circuitous in the West. There have been retreats into sheer terror. There have been equally profound expressions of the unity of power and glory, as in the time of St Augustine, St Francis, and the Hasidim. At such times the nature and activity of God were manifest. God was present and could make his presence significantly felt.

The peculiarity of our time is that God is not efficacious. The presiding view of our age has been that he is dead. Nietzsche's statement announcing this conclusion is peculiarly appropriate. It should be noted that Nietzsche does not affirm an atheism. His statement is that God is dead. This is to say that God is now dead, though once, presumably, he lived. Nietzsche believes the death of God is the price both Judaism and Christianity must pay for their persistent freezing of the human spirit, for their historical efforts to enclose God within moral, dogmatic, and ritual formulæ.

Martin Buber is one who sees the Holy as the

centre of the human situation, whose view of the Holy is essentially Hebraic, but whose concern is for the achievement of that human community in which the Holy, beyond creed and catechism, may be realized. I do not think he would object to being called, with considerable qualification, a holy fool; indeed, the holy fool in Western tradition is one mistaken for a fool, because the presence of God is so profoundly internalized as to become one with the life of the body, the intellect, and the spirit. The *Philokalia*, the explicit mystic doctrine of the holy fool, is concerned with precisely this—the restructuring of the total personality through the inner presence of the Holy Spirit, that through it man's relation to the world is redefined.

What I should like in this brief study of the life and contribution of Martin Buber is to concentrate upon his pursuit of the holy. It is a pursuit, both reasonable and intuitive, eschewing mysticism, structured out of a complete awareness of Western history and thought. It seems to me that underlying his doctrine of the I-Thou is again the pursuit of the holy, the attempt to illumine its scope, its reality, its efficacy in shaping man's search for true community and authentic wholeness.

Writing recently with specific reference to illicit metaphysical extrusions in the empirical studies of C. G. Jung, Buber comments:

> a doctrine which deals with mysteries without knowing the attitude of faith toward mystery is the modern manifestation of gnosis. Gnosis is not to be understood as only a historical category, but as a universal one. It—and not atheism, which annihilates God because it must reject hitherto existing images of God—is the real antagonist of faith.[1]

Gnosis is not merely a specific method of apprehending God. It is not a simple Manichæism, though the divine duality of good and evil has surely recurred. It is more than any religious or cultic formulation. It is a descriptive category by which the attitude of man before the universe may be indicated, for Gnosis is a view both of knowledge and of action. It carries with it more than philosophic consequences, for European culture is, at present, tacitly gnostic. God can, so the modern intellect would have it, be taken prisoner by the mind, rendered helpless by the

[1] *Eclipse of God,* Harper & Brothers, New York, 1952, pp. 175 and seq.

thoroughness of man's despair and at the propitious moment slain without appeal.

One of Dostoevsky's profoundly mysterious creations is Kirillov of *The Possessed.* It is Kirillov who incarnates one direction which man's repudiation of God has taken in modern history. Man stands constantly before the borders of death. Kirillov's conviction is that only man's fear of death has turned him to God. The sole function of God is therefore to mitigate man's terror of death. Yet, by some inscrutable logic, the present age no longer rests content with a divine vindication of death, for it has been numbed to insensitivity by death's pervasiveness. Death has become for many an existential alternative as appealing and liberating as life itself. Death has transcended life and seemingly overwhelmed it. There is nothing to fear, for God's hold on history has been broken. The great threat of destruction and damnation has been overworked. God has 'wrought' too much violence. Man can then destroy God by devising some means of overcoming his own fear of death. Kirillov decides therefore that the pure act of self-destruction, the freely willed and consummated suicide, will break the grip of God. Each man can become God if he possesses the courage to will his own death. In place of God, whose role rests on his transcendence of death, will arise the manifold divinities of men who achieved God's role through suicide. The ultimate meaning of life is located in its destruction. The Absolute is only a protective ruse, which each man can circumvent by one supreme act. Kirillov commits suicide. He has, so he believes, become God.

God was fashioned, it appears, out of man's horror of a diseased existence. Man's destruction of God is a protest against the apparent failure of his dominion. What Dostoevsky, in 1870, perceived through his character Kirillov, a long line of thinkers has subsequently intellectualized and grounded more deeply. The succession from Nietzsche and Stirner, to Heidegger, Sartre, and Jung, is an unbroken tradition of various but concentrated efforts to confirm the death of God and the bequest of his power to an enthroned and apotheosized man.

In contrast to the modern mood, classic philosophy was still able to encounter the deepest mystery with reverence. Its techniques, though predisposed to the objectifying detachment of science, were turned to ultimate reality. Plato sought the eternal harmony without which the transiency of the phenomenal world would be unmitigated in its meaninglessness and fragmentation. Aristotle, although 'purifying' Plato of his unchanging forms, nevertheless acknowledges the necessity of a first cause, unmoved, yet ordering the sequence of motion, the highest good by virtue of his unceasing contemplation of his own harmonizing perfection. However much lucidity the universe disclosed, man still encountered his world with wonder. In the *Metaphysics* of Aristotle a passage occurs which provokes Thomas Aquinas to remark: 'The philosopher is related to the poet in that both are concerned with *mirandum*.'

The Absolute, shrouded by the veil of existence, was still sought as something eluding the final grasp of intellect. Intellect was the faculty of pursuit, but not the justification of pursuit. The mystery, the numen, God, both hidden and disclosed, compelled man to search. Faith was never mere acceptance devoid of search. This fact Buber notes in quoting Franz Rosenzweig's conviction that divine truth wishes to be implored with the two hands of 'philosophy and theology'.[1] The tragedy of modern history is

[1] *Eclipse of God*, Harper & Brothers. New York, 1952, p. 62.

that wonder has ceased, and with it the passion to pursue the ultimate has passed. The mind is not unfitted by nature to the pursuit. It must achieve, however, an order of perception in which not proof, but life, is its motivating intention. By contrasting him with the God of the philosophers, Pascal did not intend that the God of Abraham, Isaac, and Jacob should be unintelligible. He could as easily have meant that God could *not only be* intelligible, or yet that he could never be wholly unintelligible. As has been pointed out in Emil Fackenheim's recent study of Schelling's philosophy of religion,[1] religious truth cannot be totally beyond the scope of philosophy, for ultimate categories must be at least rationally lucid, however obscure their content. If theological formulations are unsusceptible of rational statement, then all interpretation becomes impossible.

Buber's attack is never a direct repudiation of philosophy as such. It is rather a searching exploration of its pretensions and egoism. Buber has never actually examined philosophic doctrine for its own sake. Philosophy has always been for him an index of culture. Even in his

[1] Fackenheim, E. L., 'Schelling's Philosophy of Religion', *University of Toronto Quarterly,* XXII, pp. 1–17.

study, 'What is Man?' his critical distinction between philosophies that leave man at home in the world and philosophies which cast him adrift, is a cultural, not a philosophic distinction. It does not allow one to ascertain the truth of doctrine. Such truth, being contingent upon the acceptance of philosophy's objective, that is, the achievement of a systematic, consistent, and adequate statement of man's knowledge of reality, is insufficient to Buber's task. The concern of Buber's religious philosophy is to indicate rather where such philosophic investigation fails of the mark. Kant requires God for the moral law, though he allows him but the most tenuous existence, contingent as he is to the necessities of moral psychology. Hegel sees history swept into the current of an onrushing Absolute, carrying with it the reality and spontaneity of man's concreteness. Heidegger, accepting the 'death of God', formulates a new ontology which provides for the introduction of novel gods; yet such gods, drawn as they are into the flux of historical time, appear as adjuncts of individual consciousness, having no enduring status beyond the flux of time. Kant, Hegel, Heidegger are philosophers who variously transgress the precincts of the divine. They have absolutized a fragment of the Absolute, having made of consciousness, or mind, or being, the ground of knowledge. They have obscured, so Buber argues, the Holy which is beyond categories, which exists only in meeting, never in pure thought.

The peculiarity of modern philosophy which Buber indicates with admirable directness is the metaphysical status to which dissatisfaction has been elevated. Where once man's face before God could be described by Rudolf Otto as that of awe before the numen, it has now become anxiety (*angst*) before the wholly unknown. Philosophy has employed a reverse ontological argument. Having ascertained that there is no avenue by which God may be known, it has concluded that God does not exist. Previously, philosophy had argued, until Kant's refutation gained currency, that God's existence could be proved from the character of knowledge. This proof has faded away, however frequent the attempts to revive it. In its place has been established the utter negation of proof, the irrationality of the very conception of God, the fruitlessness of all effort to achieve clarity of understanding. In substance, however, there is a deeper source to the repudiation of God. When once man ascribed the natural order of life, the flow of the seasons, the events of history, and the consequences of moral action to the providence of God, his immediate efficacy as a being was accepted. With the development of the natural sciences and the increasingly technical character of modern society the activity of God is less and less understood in its concreteness. As more and more of human life is withdrawn from the province of God's effective concern there is less ground on which to base the knowledge of God. Medieval Hebrew and Christian tradition can readily adduce the existence of God from the unexplained marvels of the world. Knowledge of its wonders was demonstrable proof of God's existence and providence. God is today, however, the truly Unseen and Unrecognized Presence; his created wonders have been withdrawn by science and the bureaucratization of the social order from his providential purview. God no longer exists for modern philosophy, for he no longer acts. That God is dead, not merely concealed or eclipsed, is the key to the modern rejection of God. For Death means the cessation of activity. It is this, God's activity, which is no longer perceived. Buber, on the contrary, having affirmed that God is never available to logical or empirical proof, can maintain the continued, eternal activity of God. God has merely been shrouded by man. He has been covered over. It is for man to remove the veil.

# I

## *The Bare Bones*

It is extremely difficult to imagine the figure of a prophet in our society. It is probably true to add that the difficulty of imagination disallows the possibility of his real presence. Indeed, the prophetic figure is as much made by the attentive credulity of the human community as by the forceful constructions of the prophetic imagination itself. One occasionally, at sophisticated parties, plays at imagining how Jeremiah or Jesus would be received in twentieth-century New York or London. The reaction is usually dismal and the prospects of their survival dim. As might be expected, Jeremiah is stoned and Jesus crucified.

Martin Buber is among those rare human beings who are both conscious of their prophetic role and aware of precisely those conditions in the modern world which contrive to neutralize prophecy. Leon Bloy was another; Simone Weil, whatever the contortions of her personality, was another. Where Leon Bloy sounds alternately like Amos and Hosea and Simone Weil a considerably more strident *Book of Lamentations*, Martin Buber contains within his work and writing many more and balanced dimensions.

Buber is conscious that he occupies a unique position in our time, particularly in the West. He is called by Reinhold Niebuhr 'perhaps the greatest living Jewish philosopher'. This statement is both right and wrong. Martin Buber is profoundly Jewish, but he is not, as one would traditionally understand it, an observant Jew. Nor is he a philosopher, if one understands philosophy to be the use of reason as a sufficient means of articulating an ordered, coherent, and clear conception of the universe. He is not, in my opinion, the greatest contemporary Jewish philosopher; though he is assuredly, to the Christian world, the greatest Jewish thinker.[1] He is, in the spirit of prophetic Judaism, beyond Judaism, yet a judge in her midst; beyond Christendom, yet a question to her complacencies. He is not angry, though he is occasionally indignant (see his speech on accepting

[1] I would count Franz Rosenzweig (1886–1929) as the most profound and authentic Jewish philosopher and theologian of modern times. Cf. N. N. Glatzer, *Franz Rosenzweig: His Life and Thought*, Schocken Books. New York, 1953.

the Goethe prize). He is a Jewish prophet to the Gentiles and a witness of the holy to the vagrancy of Israel.

Had we been left with but Baruch's scribal recollection of the events and personalities that filled the life of Jeremiah, we should have but little. We should be able to sense, no doubt, the lineaments of the spirit as they left their impress upon history, but little of the spirit itself would have been revealed. It is extremely difficult to imagine the figure of a prophet in our society. We may hold, as with Jewish folk tradition, that creation is sustained by thirty-six secret saints—unknown, unpraised, unwitnessed except by God; however, in the matter of prophecy and the prophetic attitude, it is the attentive belief of the human community that transmutes the man of insight and grasp into the man of history, who alters by his insight and transforms by the firmness of his grasp. We possess considerably more of Buber than, alas, of Jeremiah to sustain our historical memory. He has worked with considerably more discipline and consequent prolixity than Jeremiah. It is, however, no judgment upon him that the holy spirit worked, in the days of Josiah, with greater succinctness and clarity. We, twenty-two centuries after the holy spirit departed from Israel, must explain more fully for we address ourselves to a heart that hears but poorly.

The life of Martin Buber is unusual in the record of twentieth-century Jewry. His childhood was spent in an age in which Jewry underwent three, rather simultaneous, developments: (*a*) the rise of secular enlightenment, (*b*) the retrenchment of orthodoxy, and (*c*) the development of the Zionist movement. These movements should not be seen as separate, disjunct strands of Jewish history. So far as Central and Eastern European Jewry was concerned, they were profoundly interrelated.

The fundamental challenge, to which the years of Buber's youth were subject, centred upon the rationalization of secular knowledge. From the early part of the nineteenth century onward, the tradition of emancipation, formally inaugurated by Napoleon and afterwards confirmed throughout Europe by the impact of the liberal revolts of 1848, matured. The Jew for the first time was allowed a modicum of economic, political, and social parity. The languages of Europe were learned. A movement arose to confine Yiddish and Hebrew to the home and synagogue and adopt national tongues as the language of public affairs. A Yiddish literature developed which no longer dwelt exclusively on divine themes, but involved statement of the historical and political destiny of the Jew. A Jewish historiography and exegesis, prompted by the discoveries of Protestant exegetes, unfolded a world of archæological and philological reconstruction of sacred text which shattered the classic insulation of Jewish spirituality. In the face of this profound emotional and intellectual emancipation, orthodox reaction was severe. All shades of orthodox religious opinion rallied to form opposition to the threat of intellectual secularism, but their task was made formidable by the fact that they now opposed, not foreign influence rumoured by report and distant testimony, but active and militant spokesmen within the Jewish community for scientific knowledge, non-religious studies, and extra-Jewish political activity.

It was, as well, the era in which the first tentative statement of Zionist aspiration was formulated; when some few socialist and communitarian factions actually immigrated to Palestine; when theorists and pamphleteers began to propagandize the Jewish homeland as a necessary response to the repressive measures that followed

Czar Alexander the First's fright at the liberal and revolutionary currents the emancipation of 1855 had encouraged.

It was into this Jewish milieu that Martin Buber was born in February, 1878. When he was but three his parents were divorced, and young Buber went to live at Lemberg in Galicia with his distinguished grandfather, Salomon Buber. Salomon Buber was an exemplary product of the emancipation. He maintained the intensity and dedication of Jewish scholarship, in spite of the increasing alienation of Jewish youth, the attenuated piety of liberated adults, and the narrowing fanaticism of a threatened orthodoxy. In addition to being a wealthy banker and a leader in the Jewish community, Salomon Buber was one of the most brilliant and perceptive of modern editors of classic rabbinic texts. In his home Buber absorbed the world of Biblical and Rabbinic thought and learned the refinements of classic Hebrew, which his grandfather wrote and spoke with eloquence. Presumably in the home of his grandfather Buber enjoyed his all-too-brief and trembling years of piety. In his thirteenth year, however, shortly after his confirmation into the Jewish religious community, Buber notes in a letter years later, he ceased to observe the wrapping of the *tefillin*.[1] He remarks, in the same letter, that his grandfather, although an enlightened Jew, would pray nevertheless in a small, intimate Hasidic *Klaus*, using a prayer book filled with mystic directions. The implication of this letter to Rosenzweig, confirmed many times by his own utterance, is that in these early years of adolescence he ceased all formal religious observances. His reasons for this, as for other of his departures from normative Judaism, are profoundly based, as will be seen later. It is somewhat questionable to inflate, as he does in his correspondence with Rosenzweig on these issues, the implicit wisdom and sensibility of the child. The intuitive decisions of youth, though full, rich, and intense, do not possess the formed and textured subtleties of mature rationalization. It is enough that Buber records that he ceased in this period his formal obedience to Jewish law. It was in these years, under the guidance of his grandfather, that Buber made the discovery of the Hasidim, a pietist movement characterized by intense concentration upon directness of relation with man, nature, and God. The

[1] Letter of October 1, 1922, to F. Rosenzweig, quoted in Franz Rosenzweig, *On Jewish Learning,* ed. by N. N. Glatzer, Schocken Books. New York, 1955.

Hasidim, some of whose communities were located in Sadagor and Czortkow in Galicia, were disciples of the great Rabbi Israel of Rizhin. It was in their midst that the Bubers spent many summer months, and presumably in their synagogues that Martin Buber prayed as a boy. Shortly after his fourteenth birthday he returned to the home of his father in Lemberg, entering a Polish Gymnasium, and in the summer of 1896 he enrolled in the philosophic faculty at the University of Vienna.

These were the years when the æsthetic renaissance evoked the last passion of the romantic tradition, when Schopenhauer and Nietzsche fixed the tone of philosophic statement, when Stefan George and Hoffmansthal were inaugurating their careers, when Rilke was shortly to establish the rhythm of a beauty in tension with the divine. It was the era of the lost consciousness, drowned in a sea of images and meanings, subtleties and radiations, whose source nobody knew, whose direction few fathomed. The dream was characterized by search and longing, the concrete life was one of the *déclassé*, the alienated, the distressed.

This was particularly true of the Jewish community of Vienna, few of whose members knew or cared anything for their so recently discarded Jewish past. Buber, in these years, was not unlike his fellow Jews. Not the Hasidim of his youth but the past formed of Christian saints and spiritual heroes occupied his attention—Jacob Boehme, Meister Eckhart (Buber sometimes worked with Gustav Landauer on the latter's modern rendering of the works of Meister Eckhart), Nicholas of Cusa.

The choice of spiritual influences is never casual. Influences of this kind are selected (one wonders how) by a kind of pre-rational inclination. Certain kinds of speculation attract and form one subtly, presumably because one has implicitly 'asked' to be so formed. It is noteworthy that Buber was attracted by those mystics who sought to explore the internality, the implicativeness of relations between man and God—who, like Boehme, were conscious of divine passion and concern, of the divine fire and the creative role of evil and, like Cusa, struggled for a greater whole, for a binding community in which God forms and encompasses man, while sustaining man as an accurate image of divine life.

What emerges in the record of Buber's academic years is a revolt against the complacent satisfaction of the sciences, against the triumph of relativism in the social scientific and humanistic disciplines. The decisive step in the direction of making concrete his vague, although intense, preoccupation with Western mystics and speculative cosmologists is his gradual entrance into the Zionist movement.

As Buber noted many years later,[1] the desire for a Jewish state and the idea of Zion were, and perhaps remain, vastly antithetic. It is the awareness of their antithesis and its implications which were to define both the intensity of his sharing in the Zionist movement and the limits which he set to his affiliation. The dedicated passion of Theodor Herzl, author of *The Jewish State* and the primary political theorist of Zionism, and his experience of the First Zionist Congress of 1897, renewed the vitality of Buber's concern for the Jewish community and its destiny. Although for many Zionism became the cloak of pride, the instrument of masking their alienation and lack of roots in European soil, it was for Buber the means of renewing roots, the ultimate device of re-establishing, not sundering contact, with the European tradition.

[1] *Israel and Palestine,* East and West Library. London, 1952, p. 142.

As he has many times noted, the tragedy of Zionist theory lies less in its having broken with Western tradition than in its having broken without fully having comprehended it. Buber came to Zionism a Westerner, but a Westerner to whom everything conveyed an ancient echo of spontaneity and directness that was, at root, Biblical and Hebraic. The sense of soil, nature, place, the meaning of a shared centre, the struggle for community and identity—which underlies, although abbreviated and obscured, much of Western European national aspiration—is given station in the Biblical view of the created order.

It was not with misgiving or reluctance, but with an enthusiasm that did not yet reveal difference, that Buber joined the staff of the Zionist periodical *Die Welt* in 1901. It became clear, shortly afterwards, that his concerns carried him farther than the limited political vistas of the periodical would allow. He left shortly thereafter. In 1904, Buber and Chaim Weizmann, later to become the first President of the State of Israel, projected in Berlin a Zionist monthly, *Der Jude*.[1] What they sought was a journal that

[1] The manifesto of Buber and Weizmann is reproduced in an enormously valuable source work, Hans Kohn, *Martin Buber: sein Werk und seine Zeit,* Verlag von Jacob Hegner. Hellerau, 1930, p. 296.

would address, not the circumscribed ambitions of the Zionist movement, but the reality of the Jew—his situation, his inwardness and manifest actuality, his past, and his direction. Though the monthly did not appear, its manifesto,[1] which he had helped to compose, became for him a crucial formulation. It seemed to define the motive to accomplish for himself what he was then but exhorting others to achieve—a relocation of Jewish meaning and, by implication, a reassessment of himself as a Westerner and as a Jew.

Buber attests, in his untranslated book *My Way to Hasidism*, that in his twenty-sixth year, 1904, he happened to read a statement of Rabbi Israel ben Eliezer (1700–60), the so-named *Baal Shem Tov*, founder of the Hasidic movement, in which the Baal Shem describes the intensity and depth of the daily renewal expected of each Hasid. In this description Buber recognized within himself precisely this quality of intensity and return. As a result of this experience and its consequences, Buber retired from his journalistic and Zionist activities and engaged for a period of five years in close study of Hasidic texts. The fruit of these years was a series of works, which

[1] Op. cit.

constitute a veritable history of the literature of the Hasidic movement. With painstaking attention and devotion he succeeded in reconstructing and publishing versions of the traditions and teachings of many of the greatest mystics the world has ever known.

The impression made upon him by Hasidic writings we shall consider later, but his return to the public community after his years of isolation found him with renewed grasp and concentration. In 1916 he reasserted his interest in Zionism, although a Zionism now hued with a more profoundly stated concern with the community and the sanctification of the community. *Der Jude*, which he founded and edited from 1916 to 1924, bears the impress of this redefinition. From 1926 to 1930 he published jointly with Joseph Wittig, the Catholic theologian, and Viktor von Weizsaecker, the Protestant physician and psychotherapist, the journal *Die Kreatur*, which concerned itself primarily with the application of shared religious insights to social and pedagogical problems.

In the interim of these public activities, Buber's philosophical and religious views assumed form and redefinition. *Daniel*, which was published in 1913, exhibits a view which, though it approaches his later concern with the dialogue, is still held prisoner by the traditional subject–object dichotomy. It is, however, reminiscent of the emerging principles of *existenzphilosophie* in that the relation of man to the world is seen as that of an interaction of man's 'orientation' to his environment and man's 'realization', through a deepening of experience and a fullness of participation, of the undisclosed meaning of his environment. In a sense this view is more a consequence of the initial stage of his rediscovery of his Jewishness than might be realized. Much earlier Buber had commented that the task of Zionism was not to restore life to the Jew, for the Jew, if self-comprehending, *was* life, was in effect the affirmation of his environment and the enriching of both self and environment by the intensity of his experience. By 1923, when *I and Thou* appeared, the existential emphasis had passed into the dialogic, never to return except as a lesser stage of the dialogic.

During the twenties Buber became acquainted with perhaps the most remarkable Jewish theologian and, in my estimation, one of the most remarkable figures of our time, Franz Rosenzweig. Together they shared in forming at Frankfurt am Main a programme of cultural and educational activities which, perhaps more than any other, came close to realizing the only urban religious community the West has known in modern times. Among the fruits of their collaboration were a translation into German of most of the books of the Hebrew Bible, a translation which has been hailed as probably the greatest since the Luther Bible. As well, Buber joined Rosenzweig in the work of the *Freies Jüdisches Lehrhaus* (Free Jewish Academy), founded in 1920 under Rosenzweig's direction.[1] The *Lehrhaus* was a unique institution of open seminars on Jewish religious history, theology, Bible, Hebrew language and literature. At its height it had an enrolment of 1,100 students, or approximately 4 per cent of the entire Jewish population of Frankfurt—a remarkable figure if one considers the nature and seriousness of its programme. For a decade after 1923 Buber was professor of Jewish theology and later history of religions at the University of Frankfurt am Main.

With the access of Nazi tyranny, Buber remained in Germany to supply spiritual leader-

[1] See N. N. Glatzer, *The Frankfort Lehrhaus*, Year Book I of The Leo Baeck Institute, East and West Library. London, 1956, pp. 105–22.

ship and unity to the German–Jewish community; however, in 1938, at the age of sixty, he departed for Israel, there to become professor of social philosophy at the Hebrew University. During the strife that accompanied the prelude and consummation of the State of Israel, Buber assumed a position (the natural consequence of his spiritual Zionism) which alienated vast elements of the Israeli community. Arguing with Judah Magnes, Ernst Simon, and others, that the only solution to the Jewish problem was a binational state in which the Arabs and Jews should jointly participate and share, he aroused great bitterness and resentment. It was a position, noble and Olympian, to say the least, but not designed to realize what appeared to be a motivation earlier in his career—namely, the possibility of actualization. The realities were not on his side, and the realities, whatever the force of spirit, did not contain sufficient possibilities for achieving concord.

At present, honoured on two continents, having visited the United States in 1951 lecturing to wide audiences, and having received the Peace Prize of the German Book Trade in 1953, Buber is now in semi-retirement in Jerusalem. He is at work completing the translation of the

Hebrew Bible which he commenced with Franz Rosenzweig. In 1958, Martin Buber, it is hoped, will celebrate his eightieth birthday.

These are the elements, the bare bones. The events do not mask the lineaments of continuity. There is a thread that unites each stage in the progression—from being a child in the home of the Jewish enlightenment, to concern with Zionism, to the rediscovery of the mystic centre, to purification of that centre from all admixture of esotericism and distance, to dialogue, to renewed participation in the community and pursuit of the true community and the holy deed which would be worthy of a world that is seen as a divine gift and a human offering.

## II

### *First Principles: I and Thou*

It is not accidental that Martin Buber should choose Søren Kierkegaard to underscore the tragic misplacement of the Holy in the modern world. At precisely the moment in German scholarship when the Kierkegaard renaissance was at its height [1] Buber published *The Question to the Single One*.[2] The year 1936 was marked as well by the entrenchment of Nazi power in Germany. As Buber himself noted: 'The book appeared in Germany in 1936—astonishingly, since it attacks the life-basis of totalitarianism.' [3]

When one sets out to disturb the complacencies of the race, it is useless to choose its meanest examples, for such do not heighten the perception of its folly. Rather, as does Buber, choose an

[1] Studies and evaluations by such distinguished German theologians and critics as Przywara, Barth, Guardini, Dempf, Brunner, Löwith, as well as numerous French thinkers, had appeared during the period from 1924 to 1936. See Jean Wahl, *Etudes Kierkegaardiennes,* Libraire Vrin. Paris, 1949.

[2] In *Between Man and Man.* London–New York, 1948, pp. 40–82.

[3] Foreword, idem, p. vii.

idol of the race, one who possesses wisdom and penetration, and depose him—disclose the error and describe the consequence it yields.

It is well known that Kierkegaard met Regina Olsen in 1837 and was shortly thereafter affianced. It is equally well known that some four years later the engagement was terminated and Kierkegaard determined to remain unmarried and celibate. Were this the sufficient content of the narrative it would be retained as a minor incident, unfortunate and somewhat suspicious, in an otherwise exemplary career. Kierkegaard chose, however, to make his decision of renunciation the emotional centre of his life and the touchstone of his way to Christianity. In defining the content of his solitude Kierkegaard is at pains to emphasize that to be 'a Single one', a solitary man whose contact with the world is sundered, is paradoxically the instrument whereby to embrace the world in its truth, its fullness, and its divinity.

The category of the single one is, as Kierkegaard observes, that 'through which, from the religious standpoint, time and history and the race must pass'. The elaborated choice that confronts man is whether to become a single one, or be assimilated to the faceless 'crowd'. The choice is insularity and isolation or anonymity. It is clear that the Christian paradox lies for Kierkegaard precisely in the acknowledgment that, though one must become a single one to achieve community with God, one can never become a perfect single one—there are always unfulfilled stages of depth and growth which define the ineradicable conditions of his finitude before God. To become a single one therefore is to direct oneself solely to God. The way of affirmation is pursued by the bramble path of denial. 'In order to come to love,' writes Kierkegaard about his renunciation of Regina, 'I had to remove the object.'

Buber begins his constructive reply to Kierkegaard by noting what Kierkegaard had failed to recall: it is precisely the Jesus to whom Kierkegaard makes himself contemporaneous who is the spokesman of that double commandment of the Hebrew Bible—to love God with all one's might and to love one's neighbour as oneself. Presumably the enrichment of the single one does not lie in the path of divestment and simplification but in the embrace of manifold relation. The single man is bidden to become pivot between the love of God and the love of man, turning the one into the enrichment of the other and realizing the fullness of the other as witness to the creative affection of the One. 'We are created along with one another and directed to a life with one another. Creatures are placed in my way so that I, their fellow creature, by means of them and with them find the way to God. A God reached by their exclusion would not be the God of all lives in whom all life is fulfilled.' [1]

It is not difficult for Buber to demonstrate, from this source of conviction, that a reassessment of man's role in the community and society must follow. If it is true that man's life with others is not a delusion or a diabolic temptation, it must then share in what is considered essential to life. If one grants that the Single One is related essentially to God, but one acknowledges God as existing in relation to the created manifold, then, in some sense, every man is bound by the nature of God to share with others. Where Kierkegaard wills to polarize the individual and the mob, Buber chooses to view them both under the ægis of a transforming redefinition. It is true, Buber will admit, that both the single man and the mob ought to be kept apart, but only to the extent that the single man is self-

[1] *Between Man and Man.* London–New York, 1948, p. 52.

deceiving and the crowd is, in fact, a mob without humanity. When the individual and the mob take their centre in God and one acknowledges God through the other and makes his way to God through the other, then both the single one resumes his nexus with others and others become transformed through him.

The position which Buber elaborated in *The Question to the Single One* was one developed in the midst of crisis when the Single Ones of Europe were wrapped in despair and the mob indeed ruled. It is perhaps one of the few documents of the spirit, composed in our time, written with prophetic direction to the hour of crisis. The attitude he assumed, however, is one which had come to maturity many years before and one on which it was in fact based.

In *Dialogue* (1929),[1] an autobiographic recollection intended to explore further his philosophy of I and Thou, Buber recounts an incident which presumably took place some time towards the end of what might be termed 'his years of silence'.[2] As will be recalled, in 1904

[1] *Dialogue,* London–New York, 1948, pp. 1–39.

[2] Idem, p. 13. Buber gives no actual date to the experience he describes, but one gathers from his reference that it must have taken place during the period from 1909 to the end of the First World War.

Buber retired from public activity to pursue his studies of Hasidic sources. Within a period of five years he published a number of works on the Hasidic literature as well as on Eastern and Christian mysticism. The mystic way, as he rightly understood it, involved two alternative paths: that of absorption of the I into the absolute at the sacrifice of selfhood or the drawing of the absolute into the self and the consequent expansion of selfhood. Mysticism, whatever its forms, is consummated by the annihilation of relation—either the world disappears into the One or the One is drawn into the welter of the world to transfigure it. The consequence of either alternative is, from the view of the initiate, a moment of ultimate preoccupation with the Self and the sacrifice of the world and others. It was during such a period that the following experience occurred:

> One afternoon, after a morning of 'religious enthusiasm', I had a visit from an unknown young man, without being there in spirit. I certainly did not fail to let the meeting be friendly, I did not treat him any more remissly than all his contemporaries who were in the habit of seeking me out about this time of day

as an oracle that is ready to listen to reason. I conversed attentively and openly with him—only I omitted to guess the questions which he did not put. Later, not long after, I learned from one of his friends—he himself was no longer alive—the essential content of these questions; I learned that he had come to me not casually, but borne by destiny, not for a chat but for a decision. He had come to me, he had come in this hour. What do we expect when we are in despair and yet go to a man? Surely a presence by means of which we are told that nevertheless there is meaning.[1]

This experience, recounted crisply, but with passion, was apparently decisive for Buber. It moreover contains a personal, but thoroughly explicit, statement of the elements which only later appear as principles in the view of dialogue. Discounting for the moment the only slightly ironic note of vanity with which this recollection commences (for Buber is honest enough to acknowledge the vanity of the oracle), what emerges is crucial. A human being is brought (how, one does not know, nor does it matter particularly) into one's way or, as in this case,

[1] *Dialogue*, London–New York, 1948, pp. 13 f.

seeks one out. Presumably a man seeks a disclosure whether trivial or momentous—and, quite frequently, which is at the heart of the tragedy, is so beset that he cannot ask directly what his heart knows to ask. He is met by one (whom indeed he has sought) who is possessed by the consciousness of truth, indeed wrapped in truth, who yet, in his self-preoccupation, cannot look out upon his fellow.

Buber has told us that it was a morning of 'religious enthusiasm' and presumably, on such mornings, though one inwardly communicates with truth one has closed the ear to the echoes of truth that assail it from the world. Meeting does not occur. Courtesy and attentiveness perhaps, but the opening of oneself, wrapped as one is in 'religious enthusiasm', does not occur. Each meeting, moreover, asks a question which only the meeting can answer. The young man did not ask other than by his presence, and he could not be answered other than by a presence given to him. The dialogue need not be marked by words or speech, for the address of being, of being present in the moment of meeting, would have sufficed to disclose meaning and breach the wall of despair.

The young man apparently committed suicide.

He had come to ask that meaning be confirmed, not by argument and demonstration, but by the presence of another who, having taken his centre in meaning, communicated its activity, power, and reality. From this moment (though, indeed, not from this moment alone) the change in Buber's views may be dated.

There are those critics who see the progression from the mystic to the dialogic as a normal progression, a gradual coming to fruition and statement. What is disclosed in the incident of this morning is more than the consummation of a decision. It is rather a warning of the moment, a most mysterious warning that produces a break with the past. Granting, with Bergson, the decisive character of primary intuitions which define and undercut the fundamental theses of a creative life, what Buber describes he acknowledges to be an act of grace which was paid for with a life and atoned for by an unrelenting search for the authenticity of meeting.

It is significant as well that in this incident one may date what I discern to be the prophetic concentration of Buber's career. The mystic is satisfied with the anguish of a lonely pursuit; the world, though embraced sometimes in love, sometimes in despair, is always, in its Christian statement, a thing sanctified by the union to which one may return or to which one may proceed. The Hasidic vision (which we shall discuss later), on which Buber depends, is considerably different. The world, creatures, nature, and the sufferings of man are embraced precisely because in them and with them alone is God disclosed. The world and God are not polarized. The world is no simple mirror of the divine nor God its unapproachable perfection—rather, the world, for the fact that it is seen as created world, is the manifest and enduring presence of God. One unites with God only through the world and its creatures, and only in commitment to creation may the work of creation be redeemed. What Buber repudiates, in the moment of his conversion, is the mystic way in which the unique and unrepeatable moment of consummation—whether the *unio mystica* or the achievement of Nirvana—is sought as a self-sufficient goal. What is affirmed is that man ought to seek the moment which can always be repeated. Such a moment is achieved only by immersion in the stream of life.

The appearance of *I and Thou* in 1923 is marked by the articulation of the intuition of meeting. It is a great book; perhaps one of the rare and sustained works of universal meaning written in our time. Unlike the works of other religious thinkers, *I and Thou* is not tied to an established dogmatics (unless indeed the obviously Hebrew and Jewish cast of his insights constitutes a theological dogmatics). Unlike the writing of Guardini or Maritain, Barth or Brunner, or even that of Franz Rosenzweig and the late Chief Rabbi Kook, Buber's religious position presupposes no dogmatics. This is not to say that *I and Thou* is without presuppositions, premises one grants or declines. There are *sine qua non* without which one can read little and understand less of this work.

The opening paragraph establishes a tone and a mode of access. It is this tone and mode of access which one must grant. It is moreover a tone not easily comprehended. Where it is resisted with finality the views Buber develops are successfully resisted. Where it is successfully encountered and assumed, an initial premise is granted, from which all follows.

> To man the world is twofold, in accordance with his twofold attitude.
>
> The attitude of man is twofold, in accordance with the twofold nature of the primary

words which he speaks. The preliminary words are not isolated words, but combined words. The one primary word is the combination I-Thou. The other primary word is the combination I-It; wherein, without a change in the primary word, one of the words He and She can replace It. Hence the I of man is also twofold. For the I of the primary word I-Thou is a different I from that of the primary word I-It.[1]

Many senses and values are contained by this self-consciously ambiguous language; yet the ambiguity neither obscures thought nor distorts fundamental clarity. One may casually discard Buber's mode of expression as annoyingly metaphoric or even mystic, but such would be to miss the point. If we assume that what Buber seeks is a manner of expression which cuts beneath the separateness of the world—the discrimination of subject-knowers and objects-known which are presumably required by the empirical sciences—his language is eminently precise. The world is not an *objectum* to be seized and reduced to manipulable formulæ. Such may be necessary in disciplines where utility

[1] *I and Thou,* T. & T. Clark. London, 1937, p. 3.

and application are central or, in speculative inquiries, where the knowledge derived will be converted by engineers or technicians into applicable formulæ (pure mathematics, astrophysics, or biochemistry). What Buber concerns himself with is the human consequence of knowledge—what does knowledge do to man? How does man's way of knowing the world (whether knowing be pursued through science, or art, through speculation, or the passions) affect his fundamental attitude towards the world? The German word *Haltung*, which is rendered as 'attitude', has a number of clarifying echoes which we should note. What is really implied by it is the manner in which a man comports himself before the world, how he stands, fixes himself, presents himself to the world. 'Attitude' yields, in our day, an ideological aroma which is somewhat inaccurate, for what is of moment is not how man, reflecting upon himself, determines his view of the world, but how man, in the wholeness of his being, places himself before the world. Similarly, the world is not specified or limited—it is the whole world in its panoply and display, the world that is usually perceived, experienced, loved, manipulated, and destroyed. Buber, in this statement an ontologist, wishes to find man and reunite him to the world. He seeks to locate man as he is in his wholeness, prior to the moment when each man puts on his private mask and departs his separate way. In the process of defining, it becomes clear that Buber must pass along a *via negativa* (reminiscent of the mystic's preparatory evacuation of consciousness) denying the conventional understanding of activity, experience, knowing. All such descriptive terms serve only to describe the constant conversion of the world into the realm of objects, the pervasive *It*. What the world of It, whether humanized transiently as He or She, involves is a fundamental using of the world, a draining of the world, a manipulation of the world. The world surrenders itself as a slave before its potent master. The irony which Buber is at pains to emphasize is that the slave is in effect the master and the master the ultimate slave —for the man who seizes the world, experiences it, acts upon it, turns it to his uses, wins from it only its superficial secrets—its inner meaning is never disclosed nor revealed. The world will not surrender its truth to violence, but only to the asking in which Thou is spoken.

The world is formed out of myriad lines of relation, objects are surrounded, human beings are enmeshed in multiple dependencies and situations. When one wishes to single out an object, give it special love and affection, draw it forth from the welter of its involvement, one cannot command it forth. One must address it differently (whether it be the love which one shows an animal, so beautifully described in Buber's *Dialogue*, or an inanimate object, say a precious porcelain or Eskimo whale-bone mask, with which one stands in intimate relation). The Thou is spoken only in meeting. The Thou, let us be clear, is not a state (which can be frozen and preserved); it is not a synonym for Love (the Provençal troubadours and romantic poets have no place here, for the Thou is not a grammatical device for expressing love, though it is true that the Thou cannot be spoken where there is no love); the Thou is not a spoken word (in the sense in which words are uttered and exchanged in normal discourse, for, although the Thou is spoken, it may be spoken without sound and, if spoken only with sound, a true Thou has not been spoken, for only with the whole being can a man address his Thou). The Thou is spoken out *over* being and, as such, serves to draw being together. It arises only in relation. As the I of man is formed through taking a stand in the

Thou of another, the world of It wanes and the Thou emerges ever more clearly.

Buber makes quite clear the analogy of movement in the speaking of Thou to the activity of grace. Grace, a term constricted and frayed by theological usage, describes spontaneity and undetermined choice. The I not only encounters its Thou but is discovered by it. Recall the manner in which Buber has described his conversion—'He had come to me, he had come in this hour'—and note that the Thou is not foreordained or prescribed. It comes and passes, addresses and is gone, discovers and vanishes. Each man, each single I, comes before the moment in which the Thou is present and encounters it in a twofold manner: he either ignores the challenge of grace and the Thou dissolves into an object of time and space, or the I is filled and transformed, relation is achieved, and the I-Thou, the nexus I-Thou, is realized. As Buber comments, 'all real living is meeting', so the Thou both forms the I and enables it to address the world (as grace) and the I speaks to the Thou (as meeting). It is not difficult to see the consequences which Buber will derive from this fundamental insight—the world of freedom, destiny, grace are affirmed. Freedom, for no

Thou is spoken in coercion; destiny, for freedom faces an open future in which time and space vanish before the Thou.

Buber is no fantast, nor is *I and Thou* a useless mystique. It is a useless mystique if one chooses to view the world under the continuing hegemony of tired distinctions. As Buber assesses the situation of man (and it should not be forgotten that Buber is an acute historian of Western culture), what defeats him repeatedly is his refusal to trust the world and to give the world, in reciprocity, the occasion to trust him. The world is a place of violence, for man has set the world over and against him. Indeed, violence cannot be avoided if all the instruments of human life are devised to effect distinction rather than union.

The immediate consequence of Buber's conversion [1] is a revised understanding of the religious life. If it is true that love is 'responsibility of an I for a Thou',[2] that the young man who came to him by destiny in the forenoon was to be met and the Thou was to be spoken, then indeed religion which withdraws man from the stream of life falsifies the truth of life. If the end of religion is to teach man the right way to

[1] Op. cit., pp. 13 et seq. [2] Idem, p. 15.

conduct himself before God, then surely the right way is one which restores man to the flow of life, rather than removing him from it. The attitude of *I and Thou* is, if anything, anti-mystic. Though the popular mind often confuses the difficult and slightly lyrical with the mystic stance, it is the impatience of the popular mind that is at fault. Unfortunately life does not speak easily, however simple its ultimate truths may be. What Buber derives from his conversion is explored further in the final section of *I and Thou.* If all true relation is ultimately that of an I to its Thou, and the limitation of time and insight and human fidelity and the recalcitrance of finitude constantly force the I-Thou to become, in turn, I-It, then, indeed, the perfect Thou would be that being which, *per definens*, could not become It. Buber is not satisfied with a merely formal, *a posteriori*, definition of God's nature. God is not, by extrapolation, the Thou who cannot become It (it is one weakness, I fear, in the method of *I and Thou* that God appears last and not first).[1] If it is true

[1] I am cautious in this criticism because I am aware of the observation of the greatest of pure methodologists, Aristotle (*Physics,* Book I, p. 184a): We must proceed from that which is clearer and more accessible to us to what is clearer in nature; nevertheless, by admitting this, it is no less true that what is clearer in nature may be prior in the

that the eternal Thou is He who can never become It, our understanding of God's attributes becomes considerably clearer. God is the unconditioned—this is only to say that God is self-identical. Since God cannot become It, no thing limits him. If any man could persevere forever in the speaking of Thou, such a man would be God; but such cannot be, for man cannot avoid the constricting limitations of his situation. Man cannot banish the It; he can seek only to transform it. This is the religious passion, 'not to disregard everything but to see everything in the Thou, not to renounce the world but to establish it on its true basis'.

The Thou is the Holy and is described by Buber precisely in the terms of the Holy. 'God is the "wholly Other"; but He is also the wholly Same, the wholly Present. Of course He is the *Mysterium Tremendum* that appears and overthrows; but He is also the mystery of the self-evident, nearer to me than my I.' The Holy, as Rudolf Otto interpreted its character, consists of the contrasting elements of *Tremendum* and

---

order of being to what we immediately comprehend. Although God, the eternal Thou, pre-exists the Thou spoken in finitude, only through the discovery of the Thou of finitude may one discover the never-ending eternal Thou.

*Fascinosans*, the awesome and terrifying set off by the magnificence and appeal of God. God repels and draws close. This is the Holy defined; the eternal Thou which, by the fact that He does not succumb to our efforts at manipulation in the days of our falling away, both terrifies us and draws us near. Both moments express the totality of the Holy, and the Thou is described by nothing accurately if not by the Holy, for Holy is the one term which will not submit to limiting construction. The Holy, as the Thou, surpasses the effort to contain it; and yet, mysteriously, though it eludes us, is paradoxically, at every moment, close at hand.

It is the binding up of man and the eternal Thou which makes possible the reconstruction of the world. Man cannot bind God to the ploughshare of history nor can God force man to be his Thou—both must be companions and helpers. God is as near his creatures as his creatures will allow, but he withdraws at precisely the moment when man, in his thirst to hold fast to God, seeks to tie him to liturgical continuity. Buber submits the cultic definition, the location of God in terrestrial or temporal worship, to severe criticism. Such criticism of institutional religion is inevitable, given his view, for any attempt to force man's discovery of the Thou into a fitted and unyielding mould distorts the Thou. The Holy will not be contained. It will enter each day, but each day it must be sought anew. It will present itself in every moment but only if the givenness of the hour and the novelty of each moment are introduced into its greeting. Though man seeks the assurance of God's perseverance, continuity, and abiding uniformity, it is precisely of the nature of the eternal Thou to be ever new. In stating the formula of the process-theologians, Buber comments: 'there is a becoming of the God that is'.[1] What is meant by God's answer to Moses' request for his name: *Ehyeh asher ehyeh*? The Thomist formulation [2] is patently a misconstruction of the Biblical text and a falsification of the Hebrew spirit—not I Am Who Am, but 'He Who Is Here', or 'He Who Will Be Present'.[3] This is to say that the eternal Thou is He Who Will Be Present at each moment that His presence is sought. God unfolds according to his nature, and this unfolding is what confirms meaning in

[1] *I and Thou*, p. 82.

[2] Gilson, E., *God and Philosophy*, Yale University Press. New Haven, 1941.

[3] Cf. *Moses*, p. 53. Also *Israel and the World*, 'The Faith of Judaism', p. 53; *Prophetic Faith*, pp. 28–9.

life. It is that which sanctifies the speaking of Thou, which converts it from an isolated statement of personal discovery into a speaking which is consequential for all of creation.

The world of It is augmented in each age, the techniques of manipulation and perversion are matured and perfected, violence becomes subtler, the weapons of distortion are fashioned more brilliantly. The Holy is screened off, and what light it sheds is filtered endlessly until but the merest stream illuminates the darkness. In those ages, however, where the greatest distortion occurs there frequently emerges the greatest rediscovery of the Thou. At precisely those moments when the world of It accumulates and the Word of God seems most remote and ineffective, the world halts and regains its breath. The world is constantly carried forward to an abyss and in the hour when it would destroy itself it confronts itself anew and thereby reperceives the Thou. In such moments there is renewal and a reversal of man's way. 'But the event that from the side of the world is called reversal is called from God's side salvation.' [1]

[1] Buber's use of the idea of man's 'reversal' or turning is an adaptation and redefinition of the Hebrew word for 'repentance' (t'shuvah) which means, quite literally, both a turning away from evil and a turning to God.

## III

## *The Bible and Hasidism*

Buber addressed a gathering of some twenty students, at which I was present, in the spring of 1952. He was asked by one if he considered himself 'a Jewish theologian'. His response was that he did not consider himself a theologian, but a religious thinker. He did not, moreover, regard himself as a Jewish religious thinker, if one meant by such that his position as a Jew required his support of normative Judaism and his opposition to what traditionally would be deemed non-Jewish traditions. He considered himself, if I remember his answer correctly, to be a Hebrew thinker. By this presumably he meant one whose fundamental sources of insight were more closely akin to that of Hebrew Scripture than to any other, but that, by virtue of the implicit universality and breadth of Hebrew insight, he felt close to all others who manifest its essential truth—whatever the limitations which they impose upon its authentic and total disclosure.

Buber is an exegete, not a critic of the Bible.

His task is not that of imposing upon the Bible the superior enlightenment of a detached and uncommitted intellect, but of exposing the inner spirit of the Bible. The exegete, unlike the critic, is essentially one who acknowledges that God communicates himself in the Bible and believes that, by placing himself open to his word, one may enter into the unending dialogue of God and man. The critic, on the other hand, is frequently one who, by default of faith, employs the Bible as an extension of his own scepticism.

If one considers carefully the translation of the Hebrew Bible made by St Jerome, or the commentaries of Rashi or Ibn Ezra, the great medieval Jewish exegetes, one becomes aware that the text of the Bible is first and foremost holy. The holiness of the Bible is not confused by the exegete with the illusion of self-evidence or literal clarity. Theological presupposition carries with it the awareness that God is not limited by his utterance, that each phrase of Scripture conceals more than it discloses. The function of the exegete is to draw out of Scripture the reality which its words only partially expose. The critic faces, however, a different task. His fundamental assumption is that the text of the Bible is not everywhere reliable, that its language is frequently opaque and unintelligible (as it is), that it does not conform in salient details to the observations of philology, history, and archæological finding. The task of the critic is, therefore, to separate the authentic from the inauthentic, to distinguish between the historically viable and unacceptable, and, in order ultimately to save the text, to emend its language so as to achieve conformance with canons of clarity and logical order. The critic, whatever the character of his personal religious conviction, comes to the Biblical text as a naturalistic redactor. He elevates natural incredulity into a principle of procedure. The Bible does not challenge him or address him: it is rather a problem. Such procedure is impossible for the exegete. The exegete begins by asking for meaning and, in the search for meaning, inevitably raises the same questions as those of scholarship. The fundamental difference between the exegete and the critic is the attitude of being with which the question is asked.

The exegete presupposes that meaning is of prior importance to that of textual authenticity. Questions of fact succeed judgments of faith.

This does not render the procedures of the exegete scientifically unsound—one has only to recognize that Ibn Ezra and David Kimhi were raising rather fundamental questions about the language and structure of the Bible at a time in history when the practice of 'Higher Criticism' would have brought charges of heresy (indeed, in the case of Spinoza, some time later, similar questions carried much further resulted in excommunication). The difference is that Ibn Ezra and Kimhi begin with the conviction that God addresses them. Their task is not to assay the authenticity of the address, but merely to assess its meaning.

Martin Buber is an exegete in the sense understood. There can be little question that in the period when he and Franz Rosenzweig commenced their monumental translation of the Bible into German issues of Biblical research were sharply focused.

Buber conceived the Bible as the meeting-place of God and man. God is the eternal I in quest of a Thou to whom he can speak, and man is the I who can return to God the address of Thou. The creation out of love, long a doctrine of classic theology, is here differently defined. Love is not rendered less perfect by the acknowledgment of need—it is rather that being is inadequately expressed unless it is capable of saying Thou. It might be asked why such a requirement is exacted of him who is capable of all things—whose 'I' may, as in the theological mechanics of Aristotle, call itself Thou without necessity of creation. Essential to Buber's view of Biblical reality is the conviction that God is fulfilled in otherness, in the irreducible, unique, and underivative person of man. God enters the world through man. Ask further if you will, and Buber must, as one among those trapped in the magic circle of faith, acknowledge that no proof can be spoken further. This is the underived mystery to which the Bible amply testifies. Jewish history (and it is Jewish history, Buber believes, which manifests most perfectly the entrance of God into the historical order) is a record of creation, revelation, and redemption ever-presaged, always occurring, and interminably repeated.

The distinction which Buber draws between the history of Israel and the emergence of Christianity is the core of what is perhaps his most profound work of Biblical study: *Two Types of Faith*. Here Buber explores the theological difference of Judaism and Christianity. Judaism is formed out of a faith (*emunah*) [1] in an appearing and concealing God, who enters history at critical junctures and withdraws, leaving the consequences of His entry to man's decision. It is faith which binds Israel to the moment of revelation, and only through the binding of its person to that moment (the covenant) is the redemption anticipated and the created order raised up to God. It is the task of Israel to sanctify creation. Buber believes, as Abraham Heschel has brilliantly noted, that 'sin, though not original, is universal', that creation falls through man and is raised up by man. The metaphysical split in creation, the final rupture from God (which only an apocalyptic redemption can restore) is denied. Since the relation of God and man in Biblical language is a constant dialogue of love and judgment, praise and blame, joy and sorrow—at each moment creation is broken and healed. It is man who has the task of rendering to God the sanctification of creation. In the moment of sanctification there is bound up the initial speaking of God to the Thou of man (creation); the continual historical reaffirmation

[1] See the essays 'The Faith of Judaism' and 'The Two Foci of the Jewish Soul', *Kampf um Israel,* Schocken, 1933, *Israel and the World,* Schocken, 1948.

that man is called Thou by God (revelation); and the enduring trust that when all creation speaks forth Thou the Messianic age will dawn (redemption).

Buber's considerable affection for the person and teaching of Jesus has been a source of consternation to the Jewish community and delight to Christians who see in Buber's appreciation of Jesus a modification of classic Jewish obduracy. Both consternation and delight are unwarranted and beside the point. Both witness less to any clear understanding of the position involved than to the hardened pride of both communities. Contemporary Jewish theology—Buber and Franz Rosenzweig in particular—are no less critical of the fundamental character of Christian thought for all their appreciation of the authentic witness of the Synoptic Gospels. Buber's affirmation that 'from my youth onwards I have found in Jesus my great brother' [1] attests only to the consistency of Buber's position and his unqualified honesty. The Jesus, in whom Buber finds companionship, is he whom Buber considers the inheritor of the prophetic tradition of 'the suffering servant'.

In *The Prophetic Faith* Buber notes that three

[1] *Two Types of Faith,* p. 38.

qualities are manifest in the figure of the 'suffering servant' elaborated in Deutero-Isaiah: first, the futile labours of the prophet, he who strives in secret, who is but the arrow that remains secreted in the quiver of God, readied for the moment of withdrawal and use; second, the active bearing of affliction, the transformation of the will to suffer for the sake of God into actual suffering; and, third, 'the work born out of affliction', the consummated achievement of a new covenant between the peoples of the earth and God. These three stages are not necessarily achieved during the life of a single person nor during a brief period of history. The stages, from the anticipation of the fulfilment of the Kingdom of God, form the composite life of the suffering servant who is in one the interacting person of the corporate community, the individual prophet, and the anointed Messiah.[1]

Jesus stands in the line of the suffering servants, an arrow, among others, concealed in the quiver of God. Although Jesus addresses individuals directly, beyond their relations to the nation and community, he will nevertheless speak of them as 'lost sheep of the house of

[1] 'The God of the Sufferer', *The Prophetic Faith*, pp. 155–235. Cf. particularly p. 229 f.

Israel'.[1] Buber considers Jesus as having seen the task of prophetic dialogue in the redefinition and vitalization of the relation of individual and community and the community and God. The unsanctified is not abandoned, past history is not cut off from the future, the evil is not shut away from the transforming moment of redemption. Jesus sees himself, if one can trust the primary sources of the Gospels, as yet another, in the line of Deutero-Isaiah, who are entrusted with the task of recalling Israel to its truth, and, through Israel, confronting the nations of the world with their authentic source in divine sustenance and love.

The emergence of Paul, a rigid and crystalline mind, and the contact of Pauline theology with modes of Greek speculation produce a theological statement of the life of Jesus which cuts off Jesus from the life of Israel. Jesus may well be the brother of Buber, but the Christ of Paul, the apocalyptic Christ, is permanently antipathetic to his view.

At no moment in the life of Jewish faith does Israel catalogue its beliefs and order them with the logic of proposition. Even the efforts of medieval Jewish theology to articulate a

[1] Matthew XV. 24. Cf. *Two Types of Faith*, p. 172.

dogmatics possess a rather peculiar element of inconsistency and incoherence. Maimonides' articles of faith are non-implicative and yield to no rational formulation. Each article is known to be true, not through the assent and submission of the mind, but through the witness of history. *Emunah* (faith) is an acknowledgment of the conduct of God in the historical life of the community. Maimonidean principles are at best verbal extrapolations of the lived experience of history: the superiority of Mosaic prophecy, the redemptive power of God, the coming of the Messiah are all Biblical, formed out of the continuing encounter of God and Israel within the historical order. Paul turns the living witness of the community to the life and death of Jesus, however irrational, into an object of propositional statement. In his address to the citizens of Athens, whatever his conviction of the 'folly' of Christian faith, Paul modulates its irrationality into an argument that may be described as essentially 'logical or noetic'.[1] No longer faith, but assent to propositional statement (pistis) emerges as characteristic of Christian profession.

Unlike Jesus, Paul will speak of Jews and Greeks, but never in connection with the specific

[1] *Two Types of Faith*, p. 172.

community of which they are members. The old community perishes and disappears and the newly-founded community is all that demands attention. In the strict sense the mobilizing conception of Jewish faith, 'the kingdom of priests' (that is, *kohanim*, those who serve God directly) and 'a holy nation' (that is, a nation consecrated to God as its ruler and Lord) [1] disappears and re-emerges in the ecumenical dream of Christian unity which is nevertheless consummated independently of the national and civil life of professing Christians. Individuals, not individuals as aspects of the larger corporate community, become Christians, but the community as such does not witness any longer to divine truth.

The fundamental breach of Judaism and Christianity, however diversified the implications of the way of *emunah* and *pistis*, has been defined by Buber in an address which he gave at Stuttgart, in 1930, before a gathering of four German language missions to the Jews. In this address, 'The Two Foci of the Jewish Soul',[2] he contended that the essential Jewish position consists of two concentric circles: the belief that,

[1] *Two Types of Faith*, p. 171.

[2] *Israel and the World*, Schocken. New York, 1948, pp. 28–40.

though God is wholly raised beyond man's reach, he is yet in immediate face-to-face relation with him and the belief that, though God's redeeming power is at work at all times and without surcease, fulfilled redemption exists nowhere.

The apocalyptic formulation of Pauline Christianity, which stands in contrast to prophetic eschatology, holds a view of time essentially Iranian in origin. Whereas prophetic eschatology promises the end of time as a consummation of creation, the apocalyptic envisages its abrogation, suppression, and supplantment, by a new world, different from it in nature. The prophetic sees the abiding evil of creation borne up to the end of days and directed ultimately, through the hand of sanctifying man, to God who performs the final sanctification. The apocalyptic sees the work of the end of days as the great refinement of the metal of creation, the dispatch of its dross of evil and the preservation of its admixed good. In the apocalyptic view, evil is unredeemable; whereas, in the prophetic, the evil is always to be rescued and transformed. In sum, whereas the prophetic view allows to God the consummation of his created order and the realization of its hidden perfection, the apocalyptic sees the created order as cut off from the new world and abandoned by God. In the context of the Christian experience history moves in linear progression to 'an unalterable immovable future event' (the Christological reading of Hebrew scripture) through cycles of time each of which does its work and yields to the next. The Jewish, on the contrary, anticipates redemption 'for the sake of those who turn'.[1] As Buber observes in his discussion of the Book of Jonah: though Jonah would have Nineveh damned because of her unrelenting evil, Nineveh repents and God grants that her destiny be reopened. 'Those who turn co-operate in the redemption of the world.'

It has been objected to Buber by some Christian theologians that his view is arrant activism, in which grace no longer functions or obtains. But is grace the only means that man possesses of authenticating the mystery of God? Is the dependence upon unmerited grace the sole instrument by which man testifies to his insufficiency? As was remarked earlier, it is not that God needs man, through some incompleteness in his nature, but rather that God desires that the redemption to be wrought be achieved with man's complaisance. God wills to have need of man, for the sake of man and for the sake of God's dia-

[1] Buber quotes Talmud *Berakhot*, 34b.

logue with man. The role of man in preparing the redemption of creation is carried on through concealment—each man assesses his own heart and readies it for the moment when concealment shall give way to open historical statement. The moment of preparation lies in man's relationship to God and in the power of atonement in an unatoned world. The former involves the declaration of God's presence in direct relation to the flesh of creation, without the mediation of an incarnate form, and the latter the unbroken work of history which turns constantly towards fulfilment and decision.[1]

The primary concern of Judaism is the fashioning of a way for the Holy amid the concrete. The two dimensions in which Judaism defines itself, that of history and Torah, form a dialectic which has never been interrupted.

History presented the challenge of immediacy to which Judaism responds with the spontaneous answer preserved in both the Bible and the homiletic literature of rabbinic Judaism. It also responds with the way of 'Law'.[2] The

[1] Buber quotes Talmud *Berakhot*, p. 38.

[2] One of the misfortunes, to which the Rabbinic literature testifies abundantly, was the translation of the Bible

homily is the language of dialogue, whereby the person of God is intimately addressed; the Law, the record of dialogue, by means of which God's path is charted through the concrete. Wherever Law is conceived as an immediate acknowledgment of the power of God, Law lives and participates in dialogue. Wherever Law is eternalized, as if the Word of God is formed abstractly, apart from the situation which evokes it, the Law is seen as a defence against the Holy rather than as an opening to it.

Martin Buber has, throughout his life, sought the Holy within the concrete. The history of Jewish religion has been the record of struggles to preserve the concrete against the incursions of

---

into Greek. Among other terms miserably rendered by the Greek language are the Hebrew terms, 'Halakhah' and 'Torah'. These terms are conventionally translated as Law, a rendering of the Greek 'nomos' and the Latin 'Lex'. 'Halakhah', however, means 'the way' or, better still, 'the path which man follows'. 'Torah' includes considerably more than 'Halakhah'. 'Torah' not only charts man's way through creation (halakhah) but contains the legend by which that way is to be followed. As such, 'Torah' means 'teaching' in all its facets. The legalism which has been unfortunately imputed to Jewish doctrine results from the harmless inadequacy of the Greek language, the apologetic passion of the Gospels, and the wanton over-simplification of twenty centuries of Christian commentators.

fixity and encrustation, and the pressure of social upheaval and catastrophe to insulate and strengthen the community against the threat of the concrete. By the late seventeenth-century religious spontaneity had well-nigh disappeared. The formalization of the Jewish way and the victory of Jewish scholasticism had been achieved. The course of events which began in the Middle Ages had reached, by the seventeenth century, the point of stagnation. What had been a search for the reason of divine revelation in the days of Maimonides and Jehuda Ha-levi had, by the time of the Gaon of Vilna, resulted in the separation of speculation from the study of Torah. Whereas the great *Mishneh Torah* of Maimonides was produced in an effort to crystallize the principles of Law through the introduction of rational procedure and theological system, the studies of the Talmudic centres of seventeenth- and eighteenth-century Poland had devitalized the concrete and eviscerated rational procedure of the speculative problems which made its method meaningful. What remained was a highly aristocratic, casuistic, and arcane study of legal precedent and implication. Legislation was defined for a world which no longer existed and which, it was realized, might exist again only in the Days of Messiah. There is a touching innocence, both admirable in piety and self-delusive, in the passion with which scholars concerned themselves with the study of the methods and laws of sacrifice to be restored in the Messianic age. This is the theology of the concrete (even where Judaism is most incomprehensible it is always the world of concretion that concerns it) turned on its head—for the concrete that Jewish scholasticism pursued was one cut off from the grandeur and misery of the human situation that surrounded it.

Meaningful life within the concrete is always hard to sustain. It occurs infrequently in human history and perishes rapidly. Man pushes too quickly beyond what is given to him in search of finalities and ultimate resolutions. He returns with his precious parcel of abstraction to discover that the world for which he has prepared his thought has vanished. Living within the concrete is rarely achieved through the transmission of communicable teaching or doctrine. It is learned, to the extent that it can be learned, from other human beings who, by the gesture and form of their relation to immediacy, communicate directly.

The community of Hasidim, 'those who keep faith with the covenant',[1] was founded in the early eighteenth century by Rabbi Israel ben Eliezer of Mezbizh (called the Baal Shem Tov, 1700–60). The Baal Shem Tov, Master of the Good Name, was not a teacher in any ordinary sense. Unlike St Francis, the intimacies of whose life and teaching are organized and preserved by St Bonaventura, Baal Shem has left only legend upon legend to recall his life. Although numerous pamphlets and volumes purporting to retell the authentic words that the Baal Shem spoke are preserved, each is shot through with the inaccuracy of imaginative enthusiasm. This, too, is characteristic of Hasidim—a tradition which has little use for the recorded word or the artfully recollected story.[2]

[1] 'The Early Masters', *Tales of the Hasidim,* Vol. I, p. 2, Schocken Books, 1947.

[2] A fault which obtains in most of Buber's reconstruction of the Hasidic tradition. One is troubled by Buber's conscious effort to make the stories he preserves æsthetically appealing and coherent; whereas it is precisely the ejaculatory directness of hasidic teaching which carries much of its power. This fault is partially acknowledged and corrected in the *Tales of the Hasidim,* which he prepared some forty years after most of his earlier writing on Hasidism had been completed. See also the forthcoming study of Hasidism by Gershom Schoelem, in which the historical perspective promises to exceed the theological.

Hasidism is not a teaching, but a manner of community. Unlike most religious teaching, that of St Francis or the Buddha, which press forward to community and life, Hasidism proceeds by the reverse path. Theology and teaching follow upon life, follow it, moreover, in its hour of disintegration. In its moment of assertion, Hasidism proceeds by the way of oral instruction and example, rather than by the means of written and argued doctrine.

The Baal Shem, for upon him alone have we room to concentrate, is the founder, Buber affirms, of the greatest religious movement in 'the history of the spirit'.[1] It is particularly just that Hasidism should have emerged in the most tumultuous hour of trial which Judaism had known since the days of the dispersion.

Judaism is an eschatological faith. Whatever the efforts of modern-day Jewish scholars to convert Judaism into a practical, adjustable, and fundamentally boring affair of the spirit,

[1] 'In a century which was, apart from this, not very productive, religiously obscure Polish and Ukrainian Jewry produced the greatest phenomenon we know in the history of the spirit, something which is greater than any solitary genius in art or in the world of thought, a society which lives by its faith'. 'The Beginnings of Hasidism', *Hasidism,* Philosophical Library, 1948; *Mamre,* Melbourne University Press, 1946, p. 4.

Judaism is most profoundly herself when she is turned, through history, to the future. Eschatology is always dangerous, however. When history suffers its cruellest agonies, eschatology risks becoming apocalyptic, and the yawning abyss of apocalypse releases inevitably the demons of gnostic temptation.

The seventeenth century witnessed one of the most extreme and violent persecutions of Jewry which the West had known. In 1648 the Cossack *hetman* Bogdan Chmielnitki had led a peasant army in insurrection against their Polish landlords. While en route to their objective they fell upon another target of their anger, the Jewish townsfolk, who were frequently employed as stewards for the landed aristocracy. It has been estimated that 100,000 Jews perished between 1648 and 1658.[1] The Jewish community was rent and devastated. Such disaster could not but be viewed as the suffering which accompanies the advent of the Messiah.

A people passionate for salvation are rarely patient. The wise prepare their souls and consult

[1] Consult the magnificent novel of Isaac Bashevis Singer, *Satan in Goray,* The Noonday Press, 1955, for perhaps the most profound recreation of the apocalyptic atmosphere that formed in the wake of this disaster.

the Psalter to still their anguish, but the activists are willing at such junctures to take profound and dangerous risks.

Sabbatai Zevi (1625–76) [1] was apparently a quite undistinguished person—neither a scholar nor a mystic of particular stature. Through the accident of association (his fame is to be credited rather to his considerably more brilliant disciple, Nathan of Gaza), Sabbatai Zevi emerged from the psychotic obscurity to which he would have been fated to the self-proclamation of his Messiahship in 1666 and his subsequent apostasy to Islam in 1667.[2] The catastrophe of Sabbatianism follows in the wake not of Sabbatai's enunciation of his messianic mission, but of his conversion, with thousands of followers, to Islam. The problem of Sefardic [3] and Galician

[1] Gershom Schoelem, *Major Trends in Jewish Mysticism,* Schocken Books, New York, 1946; Thames and Hudson, London, 1955, for his exhaustive treatment of Sabbatian theology.

[2] 'Sabbatianism and Mystical Heresy,' idem, pp. 286–324.

[3] Sefardic Jewry was that portion of the European Jewish population which was dispersed throughout Southern Europe following the expulsion of the Jewish community of Spain from 1391 to 1498. Many thousands of these Jews were crypto-Jews (Marranos) who outwardly observed the forms of Christian worship but secretly maintained their Jewish religious life.

Jewry, which were deeply impressed with Sabbatian doctrine, was the double problem of Redemption and the reconciliation of such redemption with what was apparently the consummate evil of apostasy. The spirit in Jewish life, to which Hasidism provided a response, was produced by the Sabbatian conviction that only by the dragging of life beyond the pale of law and continuity into a nether world of consummated evil would the regimen which sustains an unredeemed world be ended. The paradox of Sabbatianism was that it believed that by corrupting the order of the world and distorting its processes redemption would be achieved and the Messiah legitimated. In a peculiar sense the rise of antinomian heresy was intended as a confirmation that the Messiah had come, that the old world had ended, and the world beyond law had been realized.

Though the Baal Shem was intimately aware of Sabbatianism, he did not form his world in apologetic answer to its challenge. It was his uniqueness that he undertook to repair the world by accepting it. In the difference between an attitude of passive acceptance and that which the Baal Shem adopted lies the great accomplishment of Hasidism.

The first and foremost principle of Hasidic teaching, Buber believes, is the concept of a life of fervour and exalted joy. It is indubitable that all great religions have as their objective the achievement of a joy which transcends the palpable suffering which the experience of the world abundantly supplies. Some traditions achieve this joy by training man to surpass the limiting dimensions of terrestrial enjoyment, to pass out of this earth and flesh into the world of contemplation. Such traditions—ascetic and monastic Christianity and Hinayana Buddhism are examples—supply a discipline whereby the reality of life is perfected only by the seizure in the spirit of a world unseen or a world to come. Hasidism had no such choice. Contemplation in the Western or Eastern sense would have destroyed Judaism. The anchor of Jewish life resided in the masses of poor and despairing Jews who were either to be reassured or allowed to perish. The failure of Sabbatianism and the entrance of Messianic hope into the daily stream of life did not destroy such hope, but served only to redirect attention to the world as it was and is. The Messianic hope was revived. Though each Jew continued to anticipate his ultimate redemption, he began once again to prepare the work of redemption. Instead of forcing redemption (as the Sabbatians had done) or demanding of God that he act at man's bidding, Hasidism sought to restore the balance of life. The end of Hasidic prayer and life was to do the work of redemption —to do all with such joy, dedication, clarity of intention, and holy purpose as to raise up time to eternity and bring earth and heaven closer. It has been and remains the task of Israel to reunite the Divine Presence (which, according to Jewish belief, wanders throughout the Exile of the World) and the Holy One, to return the fragments of creation to their unity and integrity.

It is remarkable that a tradition, such as Hasidism, should find in a twentieth-century thinker such passionate espousal. Yet it is not surprising if one is clear about the primary direction of Buber's thought.

There are two passages which Buber has written, one in the introduction to *The Legend of the Baal Shem*:

> The legend is the myth of I and Thou, of the caller and the called, the finite which enters into the infinite and the infinite which has need of the finite.

and the other as a dedication to his affecting little book, *Ten Rungs*:

> For there is no rung of being on which we cannot find the holiness of God everywhere and at all times.

The first passage was written in 1907, and the passage of dedication was written in 1947. In the intervening period the position which Buber developed in *I and Thou* had been formally elaborated; yet there is an unbreakable continuity, the character of which we should observe more closely.

The legends of the Baal Shem are called myth. Buber here, as in other areas, enjoys his accesses of romantic exaggeration. He polarizes myth, which bursts out of life, with the 'Law'. He observes that Judaism, in its attempt to define and fix the eternal lines of man's passage through time, struggles to suppress myth. He exaggerates, no doubt, the historical and theological opposition of *Halakhah*, the definitions of Oral Law, and *Aggada*, the homiletic and folk exegesis of Scripture. Beneath his unnecessarily rhapsodic language is the conviction that the power which life possesses to fashion its own meaning and supply its own sustenance cannot be suppressed.

Life struggles to surpass and fulfil its limitations, to transform the given from *factum brutum* into *factum ineffabile.* Legend projects beyond order and returns to it. The given is no less given, but is, in the wake of transformation, now welcomed, no longer opposed.

The Hasidic genius lay in the ability to fashion a community in which creation was raised up, was 'infinitized' by the fact of no longer viewing it under the judgment of rejection and separation. The finite entered the infinite by affirming the portion which it shares with divinity. Creation is divine if it be considered such.

In sum, the Hasidic vision anticipates the universe of I and Thou and implies its essential character. The Hasidic world, which, alas, survives only in books and its few degenerated communities, was a world in which the I and Thou was spoken. The holiness of God, according to Hasidism, was wherever man chose to find it and open himself to its greeting. The work of Martin Buber is but a commentary on this conviction.

## IV

## *Man's Way in the World*

The thought of Martin Buber is divided rather clearly into three major areas of concentration: the primary problem of being (*I and Thou*, *Dialogue*, *Daniel*, *The Question of the Single One*); the literature of Biblical, Hasidic, and Jewish exegesis which historically exemplifies his insight into the problem of being (*Moses*, *The Prophetic Faith*, *The Legend of the Baal Shem*, *The Tales of Rabbi Nacman*, *For the Sake of Heaven*, *Two Types of Faith*); and his efforts to make concrete his primary insight and explore its implications for modern man.[1]

[1] In a recent essay, 'The Religion of Martin Buber' (*Theology Today*, July 1955, Vol. XII, No. 2, pp. 206–15), Ronald Gregor Smith proposes a division of Buber's work according to what he conceives to be its primary emphases. Smith unfortunately, I believe, misconstrues Buber's affectionate comments on Christianity to imply some subtle form of crypto-Christian commitment. This is not quite accurate, as we have tried to show. Smith is profoundly right in his criticisms of much theological misappropriation and parochial application of many of Buber's fundamental insights. I prefer the separation of areas I

Buber's thought pursues the joining of principle and event, thought and life. His work would be incomplete had we but the speculative writings alone. The writings on Judaism and the Bible are intended to bear witness to the historical reality of the I and Thou, the functioning presence of dialogue in the great religious movements of mankind. The life of dialogue is not, however, exhausted by the record of its past triumphs and defeats. If, indeed, the dialogue of God and man does not end, but unfolds continuously as each man asks and is answered; then, presumably the dialogue may be resumed in our day, amid the catastrophe of modern life. It is to this task, the task of showing the relevance of dialogue to modern life, that Buber turns in that significant body of his work which takes up the issues of the day.

Before entering upon an extended discussion of this literature, it would be well to recall a theme which has recurred in ever more insistent and appealing tones throughout his work. As was clear in the primary 'dialogic' writings and in his consideration of the Bible and Hasidism,

---

have proposed to his because I feel it should not be limited to primarily religious emphases, but should turn on the problem of man's being in general.

life presses to the union of community and the Holy. The joining of community, informed by the Holy, and the Holy, completed by the mirror of community, is normally called 'sacramental existence'.

In a brilliant essay which many critics have not sufficiently considered, 'Symbolical and Sacramental Existence in Judaism',[1] the symbol is seen as the emergence of meaning, the manifestation and statement of meaning within the order of human existence. The sacrament is, however, 'the binding of meaning to body', that is, the performance of an act which seals the symbol into the meaning of life and, implicitly, renders life less meaningful (or meaningless) if the sacrament is dissolved. In its individual statement a sacrament is the binding in friendship, in marriage, in brotherhood—wherein the covenant of the Absolute and the concrete is

[1] 'Symbolical and Sacramental Existence in Judaism,' *Hasidism,* op. cit., *Mamre,* op. cit., pp. 129–58, 121–48. Christian theologians are chary of this essay, no doubt because it employs one of the most charged of theological terms, 'sacrament', to mean something which is not so freely understood. Paul Tillich is, of course, very close to Buber in his thinking on the relation of symbolic and sacramental existence, but Buber is one of the first Jewish thinkers to elaborate the meaning of sacrament in Jewish life.

'consummated secretly'. The public covenant is, however, the sacramental union of the Holy and the community.

The problem of the religious community is the selection and incorporation of the Holy into the order of its existence. The sacrament is not merely symbolic appropriation, but real appropriation.[1] The sacrament is neither limited by liturgical expression nor fixed by the artificial separation of Holy and profane. The world is a-Holy, a-sacramental. Though it may be gestated by the divine and filled with His presence, it is not penetrated by the Holy until it has been retrieved from its neutrality by the community. The crisis of modern culture is that it leaves more and more of the world beyond the reach of sacramental transformation. The crisis is, in effect, the increasing disjunction of the Holy and the community; the act of binding, where it occurs, is formalized and rigidified. The world ceases to be the harvest of sacramental existence, but is allowed to lie fallow. The crisis of the world is that the province of the profane is allowed to increase its dominion.

Buber's work would be incomplete were he not

[1] 'Introduction', *Israel and Palestine,* East and West Library, London, 1952, p. x.

to articulate the bases from which sacramental existence may be reaffirmed and the Holy reclaimed.

In the *Handbook* to his lectures on logic, Kant added to the three questions which he posed to philosophy in the *Critique of Pure Reason* a fourth: What is Man? In an attempt to formulate the problem and limn the direction of a real answer, Buber wrote, in 1938, a long study, 'What Is Man?' The essay pursues its critical course brilliantly, successively examining the systems of thought which have emerged in the history of Western philosophy. Although the analysis is far too involved and its subtleties too refined to be recounted here, it is well to indicate several principles which emerge.

By and large the nature of man is seen as an objective problem in which the concrete thinking man fails to recognize that he is not only the object, but the subject of thought. Man is a thing among the things of nature (Aristotle); man is the fixed dividing line between spiritual and physical nature (Aquinas); man is the creature through whom God's love for himself is made manifest (Spinoza); man is rendered utterly alone by the awareness of his 'infinite smallness' in relation to an infinitely large and unfathomable universe (Pascal); man, but a moment in a moving dialectic of history, is the principle in which universal reason achieves self-consciousness and completion (Hegel); by a sociological reduction of the Hegelian image of the universe, the whole of man's world is limited to his society (Marx); man is the central, problematic being in the universe, and, as problematic, his final form and achievement is still unfixed and undetermined (Nietzsche); man is the creature, the essentiality of whose existence, however he live with others, is to be alone (Heidigger).

Man is either the creature assimilated to forces and destinies that catch him up in the whirl of nature or history or the being who in solitary pursuit seeks to retrieve himself from the world and preserve himself intact from its ravaging demands. In either case, whether it be philosophic collectivism or philosophic individualism, the questions of philosophical anthropology which Buber poses are not answered. It is as a philosophic anthropologist that Buber's genius is realized—for *I and Thou* is not a system of thought or a metaphysic. Although distinguished students of Buber's thought see in his work answers to primary epistemological and metaphysical questions, his serious contribution does not lie here. Buber is not a philosopher, but an anthropologist. The skein of myth which he casts over the face of reality is no less indicative for being myth. As in all great myth, its power lies in its successful pointing to realities that are not properly named. Buber is only too aware that when one names his Thou it vanishes. God does not wish to be named nor does the beloved, nor our fellow creatures. When we prize them in the relation of speech, love passes across the bond of words, as lightning might dance along a wire suspended in space. Where the speaking fixes the spirit in words, the speaking destroys.

Buber's anthropology is of a specific nature. It is a body of insight which paradoxically cannot be formulated. It serves him as an instrument of criticism, for with it he can cut through and isolate the distortions of man in the views of others, but, constructively, his insight can serve us only by its indirection. Such indirection does not reduce it to ambiguity, for its application can be indicated and described. Like Socrates in the *Protagoras*, the fundamental issue is whether the principles can be taught and communicated, whether one can fashion a generation in which man can learn the language of I and Thou.

At the close of 'What Is Man?' Buber assesses the prospects of his constructive anthropology. Between the extremes of individualist and collectivist ideologies there is a third way. Individualism, Buber contends, conceives of man in his partiality, whereas collectivism can see man only as a part. Neither encompasses the whole of man. In the former man is reduced to his being in solitude, and in the latter man is assimilated to society. The consequence of man's cosmic and social homelessness and his resultant dread of the universe has produced both extremes—the retreat into solitude and the willing surrender of creative power to the authority of the collective mind. Both distort man's nature.

'The fundamental fact of human existence is man with man.' [1] Neither man secreted within himself, nor man assimilated to the group, but rather the relation of man to man completes the picture of his nature. Both extremes, which Buber rejects, give distorted glimpses of the final truth, but both, by the extremity of their angle of vision, result in cutting off man from man. Man with man is not defined by his simple

[1] 'What Is Man?', *Between Man and Man,* op. cit., p. 203.

communal joining to meet a specific life exigency, for what binds men together is not programmatic agreement, but the transference from one to another of a vital portion of his nature—whether one call it love or sympathy or respect or trust. In any case, what passes between man and man joins them over and above the occasion that brought them together. The occasion of meeting is outside them both—it is fortuitous and chance; but when meeting transpires, the occasion is no longer chance but an event of destiny. What occurs between man and man does not transpire over neutral ground, but draws the neutrality of space and time into the vortex of meeting and thereby sanctifies the ground on which the meeting occurs. Parenthetically this is the sense in which Buber interprets the fact of God's instruction to Moses and the angel's words to Joshua that they remove their sandals—in the moment when God and man speak, what is between them is drawn into their conversation and is hallowed by it.

The objection to this formulation of man with man is anticipated, perhaps unsatisfactorily, but anticipated nevertheless. It would appear that an I addresses and calls into being its Thou in some *terra sancta* that is neither subjective nor objective, that is, as Buber calls it, 'on the narrow ridge' between subject and object. Although reason cannot cut fine enough to encompass this ridge, one must grant that the narrow ridge can be grasped retrospectively in the imagination. Surely the transforming events of life, in the moment of their occurrence, are neither viewed with the objectivity that reason would commend nor reduced to the private indulgence of feeling, but pass between both extremes.

To build out of the perception of the narrow ridge a view which human history must take is a precarious venture. Buber is himself cognizant of the seeming folly of attempting to fashion out of an institution, as irreducible to the planning board as this one, a course for human development. He attempts to do so because, as I have noted earlier, his view is consciously prophetic, visionary, and messianic. Buber does not reconstruct society within the conditions of time and finitude, but through the correcting and chastening vision of the Being beyond time and history who passes through it and prepares it for its fulfilment. There can be neither planning-board nor constructive finality to his programme, because history does not have its close in time nor may its end-point be grasped in the prospective vision of man. As a prophetic figure Buber casts himself in the role of one who holds up the mirror of man's self-distortion to his self-congratulation and the image of man's perfection to the reality of man's despair. In either role he can but ask man to trust the possibility of the way the narrow ridge holds open. In the end, after man has spoken all that he can speak, God will answer at last.

In the meantime man must set himself to his task. In this task there are two concrete avenues of realization: (*a*) the formation of new community, and (*b*) the education of man.

In the closing chapter of *Paths in Utopia* Buber expands the closing chapter of 'What Is Man?' Though it is written a decade later, apparently Buber is aware that his statement of the true basis of philosophic anthropology can be proved only by exemplification. The life of man with man, however it may be examined and formulated by the critical intelligence, is demonstrated only concretely. It is not whether man's essence is to be with man, but whether man is ever with man, whether he can successfully traverse the ground that separates him from another and be bound with him together. Having reviewed the history of European socialism and its tragic failure, Buber comes to the constructive corrective. Although the analysis of its political and economic organization is schematic and, I fear, somewhat vague and naive, what underlies it is of the order of vision.

Community is not founded. It is rather the response of human beings, joined by historical destiny, to confront a specific exigency or challenge of life. What binds them together is not the mere concern to resolve a contingent dilemma, but a concern which unites them through a common centre in which they take their stand. The dialectic weaves between the concretion of their task—the clearing of land or the joint production of a commodity—and the centre which defines the spirit in which the work is pursued. Community is therefore always religious, for it is centred not in leaders nor in committees nor in multiple individual relations that fortuitously weld, but in the divine centre whose manifest presence interpenetrates and transforms the living members.

*Paths in Utopia* closes with a discussion of an experiment that has not failed—the Israeli *kibbutz* (collective community). Although Buber acknowledges its dilemmas and confusions, the *kibbutz* fulfils the partial requirements of his conception. Not Moscow and Washington define the foci of man's future in the West, but, Buber suggests, rather, Moscow and Jerusalem.

The world is not, however, defined by community. The community is called into being; and only men who are capable of speaking the right words and directing their deeds to the right goal can realize the community. To achieve these pre-conditions of community is the task of the education of man. It is to this question that Buber has frequently turned. In his answering of it emerges a conviction which differentiates his view from both the practices of contemporary education (particularly educational theory as it operates in pluralistic democratic societies such as those of Great Britain and the United States) and present-day religious school instruction. In his essay, 'Education',[1] Buber extends the analysis we have met previously in his discussion of philosophic anthropology. Modern educators, in reaction to pietistic educational practice which lasted unchallenged until late into the nineteenth century, fear that the disjunction in such older methods of

[1] *Between Man and Man,* op. cit., pp. 83–103.

education in basic intellectual skills and instruction in the moral law had produced children whose creative vitalities had been deflected and impaired. The reaction, both in Europe and in the United States, was to pose to education the task of liberating the impounded creative energies of the child. To this formulation of the task Buber demurs. As he has done before, he chooses the more dangerous narrow ridge. The task of education is not to train the individualistic release of creative power, but to structure the possibility of communion. An educational system directed to the realization of individual achievement results in the polarization of man—the realization of the solitary, truncated individual. The press of reality creates sufficient temptation for man to retreat into an inward haven of solitude. Education is, as its origins imply, eductive, the communication of the wisdom which leads man out of his chrysalis into unity with his fellow man.

In an age such as ours, bereft as it is of charismatic figures—whether such be Christian, Jew, gentleman, citizen—in whose image man may be educated, there is but one image left to whom the educator may turn for guidance—'*Imitatio Dei absconditi sed non ignoti*'. Ultimately the educator must raise a generation that has turned its face 'towards the Spirit of God brooding on the face of the waters, towards Him of whom we know not whence He comes nor whither He goes. This is man's true autonomy which no longer betrays but responds.'

The prophet closes, as do the prophets of old, leaving a legacy of cryptic instruction. Essentially Buber is a prophet of an old and rarely tested way. As he would willingly acknowledge, 'the narrow ridge' has been trod but twice in the history of mankind—in the days of ancient Israel and in the days of Hasidism. It is a rather remote and unhappy prospect for mankind to be confronted with the witness of but two communities in the long history of man which achieve that spontaneity and directness which describe the encounter of the Holy and the historical community. It is equally true, given the premises we have described, that no other community possessed so completely or with such single-minded clarity the manner of life which Buber commends.

The difference between the prophets of Israel and the prophetic vision of Buber is the absence of the quality of judgment in the latter. Isaiah and Jeremiah are not uncertain of the consequences which await an unrepentant Israel—not merely the paralysis of the inner life or the desiccation of the spirit (assuredly these), but violent judgment and excision. The pain of failure and desertion was judgment. Only when the judgment had been achieved was mercy readied for the remnant. What awaits man in Buber's eschatology? Each retreat from the *imitatio dei*, each withdrawal of the heart from the encounter with God signals that contraction into evil which, as in the Kaballistic teaching of Yitzhak Luria of Safed, prepares the world for salvation only by destroying it the more. Although this view touches the superfices of Buber's thought, it is always surpassed by the more profound, abiding, and authentically Biblical conviction: creation is rendered evil by man's neglect and redeemed by man's hallowing. The moment of deceit, in which the world is surrendered to darkness, passes in the great turning (*T'shuvah*) of man to God. The idea of man turning from evil to good misses Buber's point and incidentally misses the Biblical point. It is not that a man turns from the evil to the good, artificially consigning a portion of the world to darkness and a portion to light. The world is neutral before the light of man.

If a man chooses to illuminate the world he redeems it by bringing to it his light, which is of God. If he chooses to remain within, cut off, isolated, or withdrawn before the anonymous face of the mass, the light continues to shine, but does not shine out upon the world. It is precisely because the life of man is with man that the world is considered ultimately redeemable.

To my knowledge there is no extended discussion of the idea of the Holy in the writings of Buber. It should be clear that no single discussion is necessary, for the Holy is everywhere. Unlike classic theology, we encounter little in his writing of the attributes of God's nature—his knowledge, power, prescience. There is no wrestling with the metaphysical difficulties of medieval theology—the validity of proofs, the relation of omniscience to freedom, the hierarchy of being. Buber does not think about God. God is the presence who authenticates life. The authentication of life consists in God's offering of himself directly to man, that is, making his holiness available. The task of man is not to draw down holiness into creation, but to raise up creation to holiness. It is acknowledged that creation is shot through with imperfection. To introduce God into imperfection is not to perfect the imperfect, for God does not meet until first he is met. The way consists rather of making the imperfect ready for God. Buber everywhere closes with a single and characteristic announcement: God is ready, but it is left to man to take the first step.

The genius and deficiency of Buber's position lie in his acceptance of failure as an inescapable element of his truth. In a profoundly important address, 'Plato and Isaiah', delivered as an introductory lecture before the Hebrew University in 1938, Buber documents the tragedy of his truth. In comparing Plato, the educator of Dion of Syracuse, and Isaiah, educator of the people of Israel, he draws the following contrasts: where Plato believed the spirit to be a possession of the wise man and perfection of the soul to be communicable, Isaiah believed that the spirit was an event which seized one from the outside and perfection of the soul to be non-existent and in utter contrast to man's unworthiness. Where Plato, in the passion to bring the truth of the spirit into the market-place of power, fails, Isaiah commences with the assumption that radical truth will always fail. Where Plato is disillusioned by failure,

Isaiah is emboldened. Failure confirms truth. Though the truth fail in the historical moment, the message of truth is preserved and borne through history.

One cannot help but feel, in reading Buber carefully, that the tragedy of failure, however acknowledged, is not truly believed as Isaiah believed it. It is not truly believed because, unlike the faith of Isaiah, I am not convinced that Buber ascribes to God power equal to his mercy. There is a resurgent emphasis, in theological circles, on the mercy and compassion of God. When the world's misery is described and the horrors of these decades are recounted, the mercy of God is invoked—God remembers, God weeps over creation (as indeed he does), God sorrows, forgives, and loves. But the virtue of prophetic indignation (which to my knowledge Buber only articulates in his magnificent Peace Prize acceptance speech to the German Book Trade in 1953) is absent. All is endless exhortation, patience, trust, and compassion. I admit that this criticism is perhaps impressionistic, for which I apologize. I have, however, always imagined that the real mercy of God will go out to the true monsters of history who, in the hour of their death, will come before God and remain forever in his

Presence—knowing, for eternity, that indeed he lives whom they have, through their lives and deeds, denied. I give heaven as judgment to the monsters. The judgment upon the 'upright' middle classes and the self-indulgent rich—all this is focused by Buber through the genteel commendation of the way of encounter. The gap which separates, however, the poverty and sharing that define the way of the poor in Hasidism and the rich, comfortable, and established western bourgeoisie is vast. Few indeed will go to Israel *kibbutzim*. What of the vast millions who can be touched by nothing else than the words of scattered men and random books? For them the prophetic call cannot be calm and judicious. Buber transmutes the poverty and filth of central European Jewish life, but does not, to my mind, retain the meaning of its ugliness. In his retelling of Hasidic stories the incidents of Jews without food or money to buy wood and Sabbath candles become folk tales, warming us on cold nights—but for those Jews life was a nasty business which they *still* redeemed. I would Buber had spoken more of the nastiness and ugliness of this life and judged more harshly those of us who can read his words with calm and detachment. To be sure, however, he protects his truth by declaring its failure in advance. There is, beyond Buber and his truth, the conviction of those who believe that at the same moment that God loves, he also judges.

## BIOGRAPHICAL NOTES

| | |
|---|---|
| 1878 | Born in Vienna in February. |
| 1878–92 | Lived in the home of his grandfather, Salomon Buber; made contact during summer months with numerous Hasidic communities of Galicia where he spent his vacations. |
| 1896 | Enrolled in the Faculty of Philosophy at the University of Vienna. |
| 1897 | Attends First Zionist Congress. |
| 1901 | Joins staff of Zionist periodical, *Die Welt*. |
| 1901 | Assists in founding the *Jüdischer Verlag*. |
| 1904 | Projects with Chaim Weizmann an abortive periodical, *Der Jude*. |
| | Discovers the literature of Hasidism and begins intensive work on its sources and reconstruction. |
| 1916–23 | Edits the Zionist periodical, *Der Jude*. |
| 1923 | Publishes *I and Thou*. |
| 1923–33 | Teaches Jewish philosophy of religion at the University of Frankfurt am Main. |
| 1925 | Commences, with Franz Rosenzweig, a new German translation of the Hebrew Bible. |
| 1926–30 | Edits, with Josef Wittig and Viktor von Weizsaecker, *Die Kreatur*. |
| 1933 | Assumes direction of the *Freies Jüdisches Lehrhaus* in Frankfurt am Main. |
| 1938 | Leaves Germany for Israel. |
| 1938–51 | Professor of Social Philosophy at the Hebrew University in Jerusalem. |
| 1949–53 | Heads Institute of Adult Education in Israel. |
| 1951 | Visits the United States of America for an extended lecture tour. |

1952 Receives Goethe Prize at the University of Hamburg.

1953 Receives Peace Prize of the German Book Trade at Frankfurt am Main.

1958 Anniversary of his eightieth birthday.

## SELECTED BIBLIOGRAPHY

### Works Available in English Translation


*At the Turning.* Three Addresses on Judaism. New York: Farrar, Straus, and Cudahy, 1952.

*Between Man and Man.* (Containing the English translation of *Dialogue, The Question to the Single One, Education, The Education of Character,* and *What Is Man?*) London: Routledge & Kegan Paul; New York: Macmillan Company, 1947.

*Eclipse of God.* New York: Harper & Brothers, 1952; Victor Gollancz, Ltd., 1953.

*For the Sake of Heaven.* 2nd ed. New York: Harper & Brothers, 1952.

*Good and Evil.* Two Interpretations. (Includes *Right and Wrong* and *Images of Good and Evil.*) New York: Charles Scribner's Sons, 1953.

*Hasidism.* New York: The Philosophical Library, 1948.

*I and Thou.* Edinburgh: T. & T. Clark, 1937.

*Images of Good and Evil.* London: Routledge & Kegan Paul, 1952.

*Israel and Palestine.* London: East and West Library; New York: Farrar, Straus and Cudahy, 1952.

*Israel and the World.* New York: Schocken Books, 1948.

*The Legend of the Baal Shem.* New York: Harper and Bros; London: East and West Library, 1955.

'*Revelation and Law*', the Letters of Buber and Rosenzweig, On Jewish Learning (edited by N. N. Glatzer). New York: Schocken Books, 1955.

*Mamre.* London and Melbourne: Cambridge University Press and Melbourne University Press, 1946.

*Moses.* London: East and West Library; New York: Farrar, Straus, and Cudahy, 1946.

*Paths in Utopia.* London: Routledge & Kegan Paul, 1949.
*Pointing the Way*: Collected Essays. New York: Harper & Brothers; London: Routledge & Kegan Paul, 1957.
*The Prophetic Faith.* New York: The Macmillan Co., 1949.
*Right and Wrong.* London: S.C.M. Press, Ltd., 1952.
*Tales of the Hasidim*: Early and Late Masters. 2 vols. New York: Schocken Books, 1947; London: Thames & Hudson, Ltd., 1955.
*The Tales of Rabbi Nachman.* New York: Horizon Press, 1956.
*Ten Rungs.* New York: Schocken Books, 1947.
*Two Types of Faith.* New York: The Macmillan Co.; London: Routledge & Kegan Paul, 1951.
*The Way of Man.* London: Routledge and Kegan Paul, 1950; Chicago: Wilcox & Follett, 1951.

Selected Untranslated Works

*Daniel.* Leipzig: Insel Verlag, 1913.
*Drei Reden über das Judentum.* Frankfurt am Main: Rütten & Loening, 1911.
*Ekstatische Konfessionen.* Jena: Eugen Diedrichs Verlag, 1909.
*Ereignesse und Begegnungen.* Leipzig: Insel Verlag, 1917.
*Der grosse Maggid und seine Nachfolge.* Frankfurt am Main: Rütten & Loening, 1922.
*Die Jüdische Bewegung.* Vol. I, 1900–14. Berlin: Jüdischer Verlag, 1916. Vol. II, 1916–20. Berlin: Jüdischer Verlag, 1933.
*Königtum Gottes.* Berlin: Schocken Verlag, 1931; 2nd enlarged edition, 1936.
*Mein Weg zum Chassidismus.* Frankfurt am Main: Rütten & Loening, 1918.
*Die Schrift.* Translation of the Bible from Hebrew into German by Martin Buber in collaboration with Franz Rosenzweig. Berlin: Schocken Verlag, 14 vols.

## Books of Particular Significance about Buber

Friedman, Maurice, *Martin Buber: The Life of Dialogue.* London: Routledge & Kegan Paul; Chicago: The University of Chicago Press, 1955.
No doubt the best introductory work to Buber's thought.

Herberg, Will (editor), *The Writings of Martin Buber.* New York: Meridian Books, 1955.

Kohn, Hans, *Martin Buber, sein Werk und seine Zeit.* Hellerau: Jacob Hegner Verlag, 1930.